THE LITTLE
SPICE
COOKBOOK

The Little
SPICE
Cookbook

SMITHMARK

This edition published in 1996
by Smithmark Publishers,
a division of U.S. Media Holdings, Inc.,
16 East 32nd Street
New York
NY 10016

Smithmark books are available for bulk purchase
for sales promotion and premium use. For details write
or call the Manager of Special Sales, Smithmark Publishers
16 East 32nd Street
New York, NY 10016
(212) 532-6600

ISBN 0-7651-9819-3

Publisher: Joanna Lorenz
Senior Cookery Editor: Linda Fraser
Assistant Editor: Emma Brown
Copy Editor: Jenni Fleetwood
Designer: Lilian Lindblom
Illustrator: Anna Koska
Photographers Karl Adamson, Michael Michaels, James Duncan, Steve Baxter,
Amanda Heywood, Michelle Garrett, Don Last & Patrick McLeavey
Recipes Christine France, Roz Denny, Catherine Atkinson, Liz Trigg,
Rosamund Grant, Sarah Gates, Carole Clements, Elizabeth Wolf-Cohen,
Nicola Diggins, Patricia Lousada, Frances Cleary, Sallie Morris, Shirley Gill
& Norma MacMillan

Printed in China
10 9 8 7 6 5 4 3 2 1

Contents

Introduction

It is no wonder people speak of the spice of life – these aromatic flavorings lift the everyday into the realm of romance. Once so precious and rare that wars were fought over them and men traveled thousands of miles in their pursuit, spices are now no further away than the nearest supermarket.

They remain mysterious, however, despite the rise in the popularity of Indian, Thai, Vietnamese and Chinese dishes, and many people prefer to shell out for a prepared spice mixture than to experiment with roasting, grinding and blending their own spices. This is a pity, for becoming familiar with spices is a rewarding experience. Learning which types are pungent and which are mild, and discovering which are your particular favorites, means that you can make up mixtures to suit your own tastes, and the tastes of your family and friends. It's a common notion that all spices used in curries are hot and fiery, yet nothing could be further from the truth. Spicy dishes can be subtle, pungent, aromatic, fragrant – the choice is in your own hands when you are the one wielding the pestle or operating the grinder.

Even chilies, which many nervous cooks distrust, can add piquancy rather than punch, if only the flesh is used and that in small quantities. As for fresh ginger, reach out for those knobby hands – until you've grated fresh ginger into a stir-fry you've missed out on a great treat.

Make more of spices: flavor your sugar with a vanilla pod; greet winter guests with wine mulled with nutmeg and cinnamon; stud oranges with cloves for a scented centerpiece for a beautiful Christmas table. Try five-spice powder, that interesting combination of star anise, Szechuan peppercorns, fennel, cloves and cinnamon so highly favored by Chinese cooks; make more use of aromatic seeds like dill seed, juniper berries, aniseed and coriander seeds.

What's the difference between herbs and spices? This is a confusing issue, as one plant can produce both. Generally speaking, herbs are the leaves of culinary plants, usually native to temperate regions of the globe, whereas spices come from tropical or subtropical plants (often shrubs or trees), and may be bark, berries, buds, flower stigmas, fruit or roots. Spices are generally dried before use. The seeds of culinary

plants are frequently also categorized as spices, so the leafy coriander is a herb (usually called cilantro), but coriander seeds — which have a very different flavor — are regarded as spices.

Both herbs and spices have long been valued for their medicinal qualities. Aniseed aids digestion, as does dill seed, which explains why the latter is often cooked with cabbage. Nutmeg is said to stimulate the appetite, and juniper berries to ease arthritis pain. Cinnamon has been credited with being an aphrodisiac, which might explain that optimistic custom of stirring bedtime black coffee with a cinnamon stick! When used wisely, alone or in combination, spices can transform your cooking and can truly be a cook's best friends.

7

Familiar Spices

ANISE

The oval, gray-green seeds (aniseed) of this aromatic annual plant have a sweet licorice-like flavor and are used in baking and to flavor liqueurs.

CARDAMOM

Tiny black seeds encased in pale green or parchment-colored pods, cardamom is valued for its pungent flavor and used in curries, soups and some milk puddings. The pods may be bruised and used whole, or the seeds may be used on their own.

CAYENNE

Cayenne and paprika are ground spices, made from various peppers. Cayenne is very hot; paprika is often mild but can be fiery. Chili powder comes from ground dried red chilies and is usually hot.

CARAWAY SEEDS

Harvested from a leafy biennial plant, the seeds are used in cakes, breads, some pork dishes and with potatoes and cabbage.

CINNAMON

The bark of a tropical evergreen tree, sold either as sticks or ground, cinnamon has a sweet, pungent flavor. It is widely used, especially in desserts and cakes, and with stewed fruit and mulled wine.

ALLSPICE

The sun-dried fruit of a tropical evergreen tree, allspice berries are used in baking, pickling and to flavor stews and sauces. The flavor resembles a blend of cinnamon, cloves and nutmeg.

CLOVES

Resembling small black nails, these are the dried, unopened flower pods of a tropical tree. Whole or ground cloves are used in baking, pickling and hot punches.

CORIANDER

The dried beige-colored seeds of cilantro, a member of the parsley family, have a light spicy taste, strengthened by roasting. Use whole or ground, in curries and casseroles.

SAFFRON

The world's most precious spice, saffron consists of the dried stigmas of a type of crocus. Valued for both the flavor and the deep yellow color it gives to food, saffron should be bought from a reputable source. Use threads, if available, over powder.

NUTMEG

Like mace, nutmeg comes from a tropical tree. Nutmeg is the seed kernel and mace its fibrous outer case. Both are available ground, but for the best sweet, warm flavor, use blades of mace or grate your own nutmeg as required.

TURMERIC

Like saffron, this powdered root of a member of the ginger family tints food yellow, but the flavor does not compare. Turmeric has a strong woody taste and is best used in curries and pickles.

SESAME SEEDS

Popular in breads and cookies, and as a source of a flavorful oil, these small oval seeds come from a tropical annual plant. They should be roasted before use.

CUMIN

Often confused with caraway, which it resembles in appearance and taste, cumin seeds come from a leafy plant related to parsley. The whole or ground spice is often used in Indian and Mexican cooking.

GINGER

A knobby rhizome of a tropical plant, this is a popular ingredient in many sweet and savory dishes and is used fresh (grated or chopped), crystallized, preserved in syrup or ground. Use fresh when possible.

Techniques

GRATING NUTMEG

Multipurpose box graters usually have a very fine section for nutmeg. Miniature graters, designed for this spice, are also available. Grate fresh nutmeg on milk puddings, over layered potatoes ready for baking with cream, and into cake and cookie mixes.

USING FRESH GINGER

Fresh ginger will keep in the fridge for up to 3 weeks, either in a plastic bag or peeled and placed in a glass jar with sherry to cover (after use, save the liquor for sauces and dressings). Fresh ginger can also be frozen, then grated or shaved directly into stir-fries and sauces.

USING SAFFRON

Because saffron is so expensive, it is widely imitated. It is best to buy the whole dried stigmas (threads) from a reputable supplier. Grind the threads with a mortar and pestle (or use the end of a rolling pin in a sturdy bowl), then dissolve the powder in hot water or stock before use.

GRINDING SPICES

Dry-roast selected spices (for recipes, see opposite) in a heavy frying pan. When cool, transfer to a mortar and grind with a pestle. Alternately – and this is well worth doing if you enjoy spicy foods – invest in a coffee grinder to be used solely for spices and spice mixes, such as Garam Masala or your own blend of curry powder.

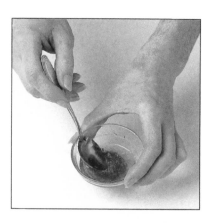

Spice Mixes

GARAM MASALA

This popular spice blend is widely used in Indian cooking, and is usually added toward the end of the cooking time. Place a heavy frying pan over medium heat. Add the seeds from 4 green cardamom pods with 2 tablespoons each cumin and coriander seeds, 2 teaspoons each whole cloves and black peppercorns and a crumbled cinnamon stick. Cook, stirring, until roasted. Cool, then grind with a mortar and pestle. Grate in half a nutmeg before using.

CURRY POWDER

Experiment to find the spice blend you like best. For starters, try mixing 1 tablespoon each dry-roasted cumin seeds, fenugreek seeds and black peppercorns. Add 4 tablespoons dry-roasted coriander seeds and 1 teaspoon mustard seeds. Grind to a fine powder, then stir in 1 tablespoon ground turmeric, 2 teaspoons ground ginger and 1 teaspoon mild chili powder.

FIVE-SPICE POWDER

Crumble 2 cinnamon sticks into a mortar. Add 2 teaspoons each crumbled star anise, anise pepper (ground Szechuan peppercorns), fennel seeds and whole cloves. Grind to a powder and use sparingly.

11

COOK'S TIP

Keep spice mixes in airtight containers in a cool, dry place out of direct sunlight.
If you must store spice mixes for more than a month or so, keep them in tightly covered tubs in the freezer.

Appetizers & Snacks

Spiced Parsnip Soup

INGREDIENTS

3 tablespoons butter
1 onion, chopped
1½ pounds parsnips, diced
1 teaspoon ground coriander
½ teaspoon ground cumin
½ teaspoon ground turmeric
¼ teaspoon chili powder
5 cups chicken stock
⅔ cup cream
1 tablespoon sunflower oil
1 garlic clove, julienned
2 teaspoons yellow mustard seeds
salt and ground black pepper

SERVES 4–6

3 Cool slightly, then purée in a blender until smooth. Return the soup to the pan, add the cream and heat through gently over low heat.

4 Heat the oil in a small pan, add the julienned garlic and yellow mustard seeds and fry quickly until the garlic is beginning to brown and the mustard seeds start to pop and splutter. Remove the pan from the heat.

5 Ladle the soup into warmed soup bowls and pour a little of the hot spice mixture over each. Serve at once.

13

1 Melt the butter in a large pan, add the onion and parsnips and fry gently for about 3 minutes.

2 Stir in the spices. Cook for about 1 minute, add the stock, season, and bring to a boil. Cover, then simmer for 45 minutes, or until the parsnips are tender.

Spicy Vegetable Fritters with Thai Salsa

INGREDIENTS

2 teaspoons cumin seeds
2 teaspoons coriander seeds
1 cup chick-pea flour
½ teaspoon baking soda
1 pound zucchini, cut into 3-inch sticks
½ cup warm water
½ cup peanut oil
salt and ground black pepper
fresh mint sprigs, to garnish
THAI SALSA
½ cucumber, diced
3 scallions, chopped
6 radishes, cubed
2 tablespoons chopped fresh mint
1-inch piece fresh ginger, peeled and grated
3 tablespoons lime juice
2 tablespoons sugar
3 garlic cloves, crushed

SERVES 2–4

1 Heat the wok. Add the cumin and coriander seeds. Toast them, turning them over frequently. Cool them, then grind well, using a mortar and pestle.

2 Blend the flour, baking soda, spices and salt and pepper in a food processor. Add the warm water and 1 tablespoon of the oil, and blend again. Transfer to a bowl.

3 Coat the zucchini in the batter, then let stand for 10 minutes. Meanwhile, make the salsa by combining all the ingredients in a bowl.

4 Heat the wok, then add the remaining oil. When the oil is hot, stir-fry the zucchini in batches. Drain well on paper towels, then serve hot with the salsa, garnished with fresh mint sprigs.

COOK'S TIP
Thai salsa goes just as well with plain stir-fried salmon strips or stir-fried beef as it does with these zucchini fritters.

Mixed Spiced Nuts

INGREDIENTS

1 cup dried unsweetened
slivered coconut
5 tablespoons peanut oil
½ teaspoon chili powder
1 teaspoon ground paprika
1 teaspoon tomato paste
2 cups unsalted cashews
2 cups whole blanched almonds
4 tablespoons sugar
1 teaspoon ground cumin
½ teaspoon salt
ground black pepper
mustard greens and watercress, to garnish

SERVES 4–6

1 Heat the wok, add the dried coconut and dry-fry until golden. Let cool.

2 Heat the wok and add 3 tablespoons of the peanut oil. When the oil is hot, add the chili, paprika and tomato paste. Gently stir-fry the cashews in the spicy mix until well coated. Drain well and season. Let cool.

3 Wipe the inside of the wok with paper towels, heat it, then add the remaining oil. When the oil is hot, add the blanched almonds and sprinkle in  the sugar. Stir-fry gently until the almonds are golden and the sugar is caramelized. Place the cumin and salt in a bowl. Add the almonds, toss well, then set aside to cool.

4 Stir the cashews, almonds and slivered coconut together or serve in separate bowls. Garnish with mustard greens and watercress.

16

Spicy Meat Patties with Coconut

INGREDIENTS

*1⅓ cups freshly grated coconut, or
slivered coconut soaked in
4-6 tablespoons boiling water
1½ cups finely ground beef
½ teaspoon each coriander and cumin seeds,
dry-fried
1 garlic clove, crushed
a little beaten egg
1-2 tablespoons flour
peanut oil, for frying
salt
thin lemon and lime wedges, to serve*

MAKES 22

1 Combine the coconut and the beef in a mixing bowl and set aside. (It is not necessary to add water if using fresh coconut.)

3 Divide the meat into equal portions the size of a walnut, and form into patties. Dust the patties lightly with flour.

2 Grind the dry-fried coriander and cumin seeds with a mortar and pestle. Add to the meat mixture with the garlic, salt to taste, and enough beaten egg to bind.

4 Heat the oil and then fry the patties for 4–5 minutes until both sides are golden brown and cooked through. Serve with lemon and lime wedges, to squeeze over.

Plantain Chips

INGREDIENTS

vegetable oil, for shallow frying
2 green plantains
½ onion
1 yellow plantain
pinch of garlic powder
cayenne pepper
salt

SERVES 4

18

2 Fry the plantain rounds in the oil for about 3 minutes, turning until golden brown. Drain on paper towels and keep hot in a low oven.

3 Coarsely grate the other green plantain and put on a plate. Slice the onion into wafer-thin shreds with a sharp knife and mix with the grated plantain.

4 Heat a little more oil in the frying pan and fry handfuls of the onion mixture for 2–3 minutes, until golden, turning once. Drain and keep hot.

5 Heat a little more oil in the frying pan and, while it is heating, peel the yellow plantain, cut in half lengthwise and dice. Sprinkle with the garlic powder and cayenne. Fry until golden brown, turning to brown evenly. Drain on paper towels and then arrange the three varieties of cooked plantains in shallow dishes. Sprinkle with salt and serve.

I Heat the oil in a large frying pan over medium heat. While the oil is heating, peel one of the green plantains and pare thinly into very neat rounds.

Spicy Kebabs

INGREDIENTS

1 pound sirloin
½ teaspoon sugar
1 teaspoon garlic powder
1 teaspoon ground ginger
1 teaspoon paprika
1 teaspoon ground cinnamon
pinch of chili powder
2 teaspoons onion salt
½ cup peanuts, finely crushed
vegetable oil, for brushing
red onion rings, to garnish (optional)

SERVES 4

1 Trim the steak of any fat and then cut into 1-inch-wide strips. Place in a bowl or a shallow dish and chill until needed.

2 Mix the sugar, garlic powder, spices and onion salt together in a small bowl with the crushed nuts. Mix well, then press the mixture into the steak.

3 Thread all the spicy steak onto eight satay sticks. Push the strips together closely. Place the kebabs in a shallow dish, cover them loosely with foil and let them marinate in a cool place for a few hours to allow the flavors to develop.

4 Preheat a broiler or barbecue. Brush the meat with a little oil and then cook at medium heat for about 15 minutes, until evenly browned. Turn the kebabs frequently to cook them evenly. Serve immediately, with red onion rings, if desired.

Spiced Honey Chicken Wings

INGREDIENTS

1 red chili, finely chopped
1 teaspoon chili powder
1 teaspoon ground ginger
rind of 1 lime, finely grated
12 chicken wings
4 tablespoons sunflower oil
1 tablespoon chopped fresh cilantro
2 tablespoons soy sauce
3 tablespoons honey
lime slices, to serve

SERVES 4

1 Mix the fresh chili, chili powder, ground ginger and the lime rind together. Rub the mixture into the chicken wings and chill for at least 2 hours.

2 Heat half the oil in a wok. When it is hot, add half the wings. Fry for 10 minutes, turning often, until crisp and golden. Drain on paper towels. Repeat with the remaining oil and chicken wings.

3 Add the cilantro to the hot wok and stir-fry for 30 seconds, then return the wings to the wok and stir-fry the mixture for 1 minute more.

4 Stir in the soy sauce and honey, and stir-fry for 1 minute. Serve the spiced honey chicken wings at once, with the lime slices to squeeze over the top.

Fish Dishes

Cajun Spiced Fish

INGREDIENTS

1 teaspoon dried thyme
1 teaspoon dried oregano
1 teaspoon ground black pepper
¼ teaspoon cayenne pepper
2 teaspoons paprika
½ teaspoon garlic salt
4 tail-end pieces cod fillet,
about 6 ounces each
6 tablespoons butter
½ red bell pepper, sliced
½ green bell pepper, sliced
fresh thyme, to garnish
brioled tomatoes and mashed sweet
potato, to serve

SERVES 4

23

1 Place all the herbs and spices in a bowl and mix well. Dip the fish fillets in the spice mixture until they are lightly coated. Heat 2 tablespoons of the butter in a large frying pan, add the peppers and fry for 4–5 minutes, or until softened. Remove the peppers and keep hot in a low oven.

2 Add the rest of the butter to the pan and heat until sizzling. Add the fish fillets and fry over medium heat for 3–4 minutes on each side, until they are browned.

3 Transfer the fish to a warmed serving dish and surround with the peppers. Garnish with thyme. Serve the spiced fish with some broiled tomatoes and plenty of mashed sweet potato.

Spiced Salmon Stir-fry

INGREDIENTS

4 salmon steaks, about 8 ounces each
4 whole star anise
1 dried red chili, seeded (optional)
2 sticks of lemongrass, sliced
finely grated rind and juice of 3 limes
2 tablespoons honey
2 tablespoons grapeseed oil
salt and ground black pepper
lime wedges, to garnish

SERVES 4

1 Remove the middle bone from each salmon steak using a very sharp filleting knife, to make two neat strips from each piece of fish.

2 Holding the fish firmly, neatly cut off the skin – a little salt on your fingers may help your grip. Cut the fish into pieces, if desired, and place it in a glass bowl.

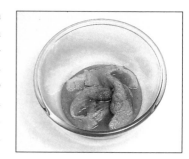

3 Coarsely crush the star anise with a mortar and pestle, with the chili, if using. Add to the salmon with the lemongrass, lime rind and juice, and honey, and toss to coat. Season well with salt and pepper, cover and place in the fridge to marinate overnight.

4 Carefully drain the salmon, reserving all the marinade, and pat dry with paper towels.

5 Heat a wok, then add the oil. When the oil is hot, add the salmon and stir-fry, stirring constantly until cooked. Increase the heat, pour on the lime marinade and bring to a boil. Serve immediately, with a garnish of lime wedges.

COOK'S TIP

Marinating the salmon allows all the flavors to develop, and the lime tenderizes the fish beautifully, so it needs very little stir-frying. Be careful not to overcook it.

Louisiana Cod

INGREDIENTS

2 tablespoons plain yogurt
1 tablespoon lemon or lime juice
4 cod steaks, about 6 ounces each
1 garlic clove, crushed
1 teaspoon ground cumin
1 teaspoon paprika
1 teaspoon mustard powder
½ teaspoon cayenne pepper
½ teaspoon dried thyme
½ teaspoon dried oregano
lemon slices, to garnish
new potatoes and a green salad, to serve

SERVES 4

1 Mix the yogurt and lemon juice and brush lightly over the fish. Combine the garlic, spices and herbs and rub into both sides of the fish, coating well.

2 Lightly grease a ridged broiler pan or heavy frying pan. Heat until very hot. Add the fish and cook over high heat for 4 minutes, or until the underside of each steak is well browned.

3 Turn over the cod steaks and cook for 4 more minutes, or until they have cooked through. Garnish with lemon slices and serve immediately, with new potatoes and salad.

COOK'S TIP

This recipe works equally well with any firm-fleshed fish, such as swordfish, shark, tuna or halibut.

26

Spicy Crab & Coconut

INGREDIENTS

½ cup dried unsweetened
slivered coconut
2 garlic cloves
2-inch piece fresh ginger, peeled and grated
½ teaspoon cumin seeds
1 small cinnamon stick
½ teaspoon ground turmeric
2 dried red chilies
1 tablespoon coriander seeds
½ teaspoon poppy seeds
1 tablespoon vegetable oil
1 onion, sliced
1 small green bell pepper, cut into strips
16 crab claws
fresh cilantro sprigs,
to garnish
⅔ cup plain yogurt,
to serve (optional)

SERVES 4

1 Place the coconut, garlic, ginger, cumin seeds, cinnamon, turmeric, red chilies, coriander and poppy seeds in a food processor and process until well blended.

2 Heat the oil in a wok and fry the onion until soft, but not colored. Add the green pepper.

3 Stir in the spice mixture and stir-fry for 1 minute.

4 Remove all the vegetables with a slotted spoon. Heat the wok. Add the crab claws, stir-fry for 2 minutes, then briefly return all the spiced vegetables to the wok  and heat through. Garnish with fresh cilantro sprigs and serve with yogurt, if desired.

Fish Curry

INGREDIENTS

1½ pounds white boneless fish such as halibut,
cod or monkfish
juice of ½ lime
1 teaspoon cider vinegar
2⅔ cups grated fresh coconut
1-inch piece fresh ginger, peeled
and grated
6 garlic cloves
1 pound tomatoes, chopped
3 tablespoons sunflower oil
12 ounces onions, roughly chopped
20 curry leaves
1 teaspoon ground coriander
½ teaspoon ground turmeric
2 teaspoons chili powder
1¼ cups water
½ teaspoon cumin seeds
½ teaspoon fenugreek seeds
salt and ground black pepper
lime slices and fresh coconut slivers, to garnish

SERVES 4

1 Marinate the fish in a shallow bowl, in the lime juice, vinegar and a pinch of salt, for 30 minutes.

2 In a food processor fitted with a metal blade, process the grated coconut, ginger, garlic cloves and tomatoes to make a paste.

3 Heat the oil in a frying pan, add the onions and cook until golden brown, then add the curry leaves.

4 Add the ground coriander, turmeric and chili powder and stir-fry for 1 minute.

5 Add the coconut paste and cook for 3–4 minutes, stirring constantly. Pour in the water, bring to a boil, lower the heat and simmer for 4 minutes.

6 In the mean-time, pound the cumin seeds and fenugreek together with a mortar and pestle. Lay the fish on top of the sauce in the frying pan, sprinkle it  evenly with the fenugreek mixture and cook for about 15 minutes, or until the fish is tender. Lift out the fish, chop it into bite-size pieces and return them to the sauce. Heat through briefly, then serve, garnished with the lime slices and fresh coconut.

28

Lobster Piri Piri

INGREDIENTS

4 tablespoons vegetable oil
2 onions, chopped
1 teaspoon chopped fresh ginger
1 pound fresh or canned tomatoes, chopped
1 tablespoon tomato paste
8 ounces peeled cooked shrimp
2 teaspoons ground coriander
1 green chili, seeded and chopped
1 tablespoon ground dried shrimp
or crayfish
1 green bell pepper, seeded and sliced
2½ cups water
2 cooked lobsters, halved
salt and ground black pepper
fresh cilantro sprigs, to garnish
white rice, to serve

SERVES 2–4

1 To make the sauce, heat the oil in a large pan, add the onions, ginger, tomatoes and the tomato paste. Fry gently for 5 minutes, or until the onions are tender.

2 Add the shrimp, ground coriander, chili and ground shrimp and stir well to mix.

3 Stir in the green pepper, water and salt and pepper. Bring to a boil and let simmer, uncovered, over medium heat for 20–30 minutes until thickened.

4 Pour the sauce into a flameproof casserole and add the lobsters. Heat through. Arrange the lobster halves on a bed of rice on 2–4 warmed serving plates and pour the sauce over each portion. Garnish with a few cilantro sprigs and serve piping hot.

Meat Dishes

Moroccan Spiced Rock Cornish Hens

INGREDIENTS

1 cup cooked long-grain rice
1 small onion, finely chopped
finely grated rind and juice of 1 lemon
2 tablespoons chopped fresh mint
3 tablespoons chopped dried apricots
2 tablespoons plain yogurt
2 teaspoons ground turmeric
2 teaspoons ground cumin
2 Rock Cornish game hens (1 pound each)
salt and ground black pepper
lemon slices and mint sprigs, to garnish
mixed rice and wild rice, to serve

SERVES 4

1 Preheat the oven to 400°F. Combine the rice, onion, lemon rind, mint and apricots. Stir in half each of the lemon juice, yogurt, turmeric and cumin, and season with salt and pepper.

2 Stuff both the hens with the rice mixture at the neck end only. Any spare stuffing can be cooked in a dish. Place the hens on a rack in a roasting pan.

3 Combine the remaining lemon juice, yogurt, turmeric and cumin, then brush it over the hens. Cover the birds loosely with aluminum foil and roast for 30 minutes.

4 Remove the foil and roast for 15 more minutes until the birds are golden brown and the juices run clear, not pink, when the thighs are pierced. Cut each bird in half with a sharp knife or poultry shears, and serve with the extra stuffing or a mixture of rice and wild rice. Garnish with lemon slices and fresh mint sprigs.

33

Roast Wild Duck with Juniper

INGREDIENTS

*1 tablespoon juniper berries, fresh
if possible
1 oven-ready wild duck (preferably a mallard)
2 tablespoons butter, softened
3 tablespoons gin
½ cup duck or chicken stock
½ cup heavy or whipping cream
salt and ground black pepper
watercress, to garnish*

SERVES 2

1 Preheat the oven to 450°F. Reserve a few juniper berries for garnishing and put the remainder in a heavy plastic bag. Crush the berries coarsely with a rolling pin.

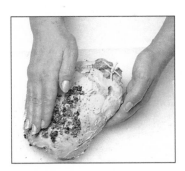

2 Wipe the duck with damp paper towels and remove any excess fat or skin. Spread with butter and season well, then pat all over with the crushed berries.

3 Place the duck in a roasting pan and roast for 20–25 minutes, basting occasionally; the juices should run slightly pink when the thigh is pierced with a knife. Pour the juices from the cavity into the roasting pan and transfer the duck to a carving board. Cover with foil; let sit for 10–15 minutes.

4 Meanwhile, skim off most of the fat from the roasting pan, leaving as many of the juniper berries as possible, and place the pan over medium-high heat. Add the gin. Stir, scraping the base of the pan. Bring to a boil. Cook until the liquid has almost evaporated, then add the stock and boil to reduce by half. Add the cream and boil for 2 more minutes, or until the sauce thickens slightly. Strain into a small saucepan and keep warm.

5 Carve the legs from the duck and separate the thigh from the drumstick. Remove the breasts and arrange the duck in a warmed serving dish. Pour a little sauce over it, sprinkle it with the reserved juniper berries and garnish with watercress.

COOK'S TIP

If you do not serve the legs, use the legs and duck carcass to make a duck stock for use in other game dishes.

34

Chicken in Spicy Yogurt

INGREDIENTS

6 chicken pieces
juice of 1 lemon
1 teaspoon salt
MARINADE
1 teaspoon coriander seeds
2 teaspoons cumin seeds
6 cloves
2 bay leaves
1 onion, quartered
2 garlic cloves
2-inch piece fresh ginger, peeled
and roughly chopped
½ teaspoon chili powder
1 teaspoon turmeric
⅔ cup plain yogurt
lemon wedges and mint sprigs, to garnish
mixed salad leaves, to serve

SERVES 6

1 Skin the chicken pieces and make deep slashes in the fleshiest parts with a sharp knife. Place in a shallow dish, sprinkle on the lemon juice and salt, and rub in well.

2 Make the marinade. Spread the coriander and cumin seeds, cloves and bay leaves in a large frying pan and dry-fry until the bay leaves are crisp.

3 Cool the spices and grind them coarsely in a mortar with a pestle.

4 Finely chop the onion, garlic and ginger in a food processor or blender. Add the ground spices, chili powder, turmeric and yogurt, then strain in the lemon juice from the chicken.

5 Arrange all the chicken pieces in a single layer in a roasting pan. Pour on the marinade, then cover and chill for 24–36 hours, regularly turning the chicken pieces.

6 Preheat the oven to 400°F. Cook the chicken for 45 minutes. Serve hot or cold, garnished with slices of lemon and fresh mint, accompanied by a few mixed salad leaves.

VARIATION
This marinade will also work well brushed over skewers of lamb or pork fillet.

36

Pork Roasted with Herbs, Spices & Rum

INGREDIENTS

2 garlic cloves, crushed
3 tablespoons soy sauce
1 tablespoon malt vinegar
1 tablespoon finely chopped celery
2 tablespoons chopped scallion
1½ teaspoons dried thyme
1 teaspoon dried sage
½ teaspoon pumpkin pie spice
1 tablespoon raw sugar
2 teaspoons curry powder
½ cup rum
1 pork loin (3-3½ pounds), boned and scored
salt and ground black pepper
scallion curls, to garnish
SAUCE
2 tablespoons butter or margarine
1 tablespoon tomato paste
1¼ cups stock
1 tablespoon chopped fresh parsley
1 tablespoon raw sugar
Tabasco sauce, to taste
salt

SERVES 6—8

1 Combine the garlic, soy sauce, vinegar, celery, scallion, thyme, sage, pumpkin pie spice, raw sugar, curry powder, rum, and salt and pepper.

2 Open out the pork. Slash the meat but do not cut it through. Spread the spice mixture all over the meat and press it in well. Chill overnight.

3 Preheat the oven to 375°F. Roll the meat up, then tie tightly in several places with strong cotton string to hold it in place. Spread a large piece of foil across a roasting pan and place the pork in the center. Baste the pork with a few spoonfuls of the marinade and wrap the foil around it, holding in the marinade.

4 Bake in the oven for 1¾ hours, then remove the foil, baste with any remaining marinade and cook for 1 more hour. Check occasionally that the pork is not drying out, and baste with any pan juices.

5 Transfer the pork to a warmed serving dish and let stand in a warm place for 15 minutes before serving. Meanwhile, make the sauce. Pour the pan juices into a small saucepan, add the butter or margarine, the tomato paste, stock, parsley, sugar, Tabasco and salt to taste. Simmer gently until reduced. Serve the pork sliced, garnished with scallion curls. Pass the sauce separately.

Steak au Poivre

INGREDIENTS

2 tablespoons black peppercorns
2 fillet or sirloin steaks, about 8 ounces each
1 tablespoon butter
2 teaspoons vegetable oil
3 tablespoons brandy
⅔ cup whipping cream
1 garlic clove, finely chopped
salt, if needed

SERVES 2

40

2 Put the steaks on a board. Press the pepper onto both sides of the meat, coating it completely.

3 Melt the butter with the oil in a heavy frying pan over medium-high heat. Add the meat and cook, turning once, until done as desired (rare meat will still be fairly soft when pressed, medium-rare will be slightly soft, medium will be springy and well-done, firm). Transfer the steaks to a warmed platter or plates and cover with foil to keep them hot.

4 Pour in the brandy to deglaze the pan. Allow to boil until reduced by half, scraping the bottom of the pan, then add the cream and garlic. Boil gently over medium heat for about 4 minutes, until the cream is reduced by one-third. Stir any accumulated juices from the meat into the sauce, taste and add salt, if necessary. Serve the steaks with the brandy and cream sauce.

1 Place the black peppercorns in a plastic bag. Crush with a rolling pin or the bottom of a heavy pan until medium-coarse, or crush in a mortar with a pestle.

Moroccan Lamb Stew

INGREDIENTS

4 tablespoons olive oil
2 teaspoons sugar
2 teaspoons ground cumin
1 teaspoon ground cinnamon
1 teaspoon ground ginger
½ teaspoon ground turmeric
½ teaspoon powdered saffron or paprika
3 pounds lamb shoulder, trimmed of all fat
and cut into 2-inch pieces
2 onions, coarsely chopped
3 garlic cloves, finely chopped
1 cup lamb stock
2 tomatoes, peeled, seeded and chopped
15-ounce can chick-peas, drained
⅔ cup raisins, soaked in warm water to cover
for 10 minutes
10-24 pitted black olives,
such as Kalamata
2 preserved lemons, thinly sliced, or grated
rind of 1 unwaxed lemon
4-6 tablespoons chopped fresh cilantro
salt and ground black pepper
steamed couscous, to serve

SERVES 6–8

1 In a large bowl, combine half the olive oil with the sugar, cumin, cinnamon, ginger, turmeric, saffron or paprika, pepper and 1 teaspoon salt.

2 Add the lamb to the spice mixture, toss to coat well and set aside for at least 20 minutes to allow the flavors to develop.

3 Heat the remaining oil in a large heavy frying pan. Brown the lamb pieces evenly, in batches, then transfer to a large flameproof casserole.

4 Add the onions to the frying pan and stir them until well browned. Stir in the garlic, stock and chopped tomatoes. Pour into the casserole, add water to cover and bring to a boil over high heat, skimming any foam that rises to the top. Reduce the heat to low and simmer for about 1 hour, or until the meat is tender.

5 Add the chick-peas to the lamb in the casserole with about 1 cup water. Stir in the raisins and their soaking liquid and simmer for 30 minutes. Stir in the olives  and sliced preserved lemons or lemon rind and simmer for 20–30 minutes more. Stir in half the chopped fresh cilantro. To serve, spoon the steamed couscous onto a warmed serving dish, spoon the lamb stew on top and sprinkle with the remaining fresh cilantro.

Desserts

Spiced Nutty Bananas

INGREDIENTS

6 ripe but firm bananas
2 tablespoons chopped unsalted cashews
2 tablespoons chopped unsalted peanuts
2 tablespoons dried coconut
½–1 tablespoon raw sugar
1 teaspoon ground cinnamon, plus extra
for dusting
½ teaspoon freshly grated nutmeg
4 tablespoons rum
⅔ cup orange juice
1 tablespoon butter
sour cream or heavy cream, to serve

SERVES 3

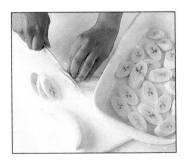

1 Preheat the oven to 400°F. Slice the bananas and place them in a greased, shallow ovenproof dish. Combine the cashews, peanuts, coconut, raw sugar, cinnamon and nutmeg in a mixing bowl. Pour the rum and juice over the bananas; sprinkle with the nut mix.

2 Dot the top with butter, then bake in the oven for 15–20 minutes, or until the bananas are golden and the sauce is bubbly. Serve at once with sour cream, dusted with cinnamon.

COOK'S TIP
Freshly grated nutmeg makes all the difference in this dish. More rum can be added if you like. Chopped mixed nuts can be used instead of cashews and peanuts.

Cinnamon & Apricot Soufflés

INGREDIENTS

3 eggs
½ cup apricot jam
finely grated rind of ½ lemon
1 teaspoon ground cinnamon, plus extra
to decorate
flour, for dusting

SERVES 4

46

3 Place the egg whites in a clean bowl and whisk them until they are stiff enough to hold soft peaks.

4 Using a metal spoon or spatula, fold the egg whites evenly into the yolk mixture, taking care to knock out as little air as possible.

5 Divide the spicy soufflé mixture between the prepared dishes and bake for 10–15 minutes, or until well-risen and pale gold on the top. Place each soufflé dish on an individual plate and serve at once, dusted with a little extra ground cinnamon.

1 Preheat the oven to 375°F. Lightly grease four individual soufflé dishes and dust them with a light coating of flour.

2 Separate the eggs and place the yolks in a bowl with the jam, lemon rind and cinnamon. Whisk hard until the mixture is very thick and pale.

COOK'S TIP

Puréed fresh or well-drained canned apricots can be used instead of the apricot jam, but make sure the mixture is not too wet, or the soufflé will not rise properly. Also, try using other fruits, such as fresh or canned pears or peaches.

Ginger Baked Pears

INGREDIENTS

4 large pears
1¼ cups heavy or whipping cream
¼ cup sugar
½ teaspoon vanilla extract
¼ teaspoon ground cinnamon
pinch of freshly grated nutmeg
1 teaspoon grated fresh ginger

SERVES 4

48

1 Preheat the oven to 375°F. Lightly butter a large shallow baking dish.

2 Peel the pears, cut in half lengthwise and remove the cores. Arrange, cut-side down, in a single layer in the baking dish. Mix the cream with the sugar and vanilla extract. Add the cinnamon, nutmeg and ginger and pour the mixture over the pears.

3 Bake for 30–35 minutes, basting from time to time, until the pears are tender and browned on top and the cream is thick and bubbly. Set aside to cool slightly before serving.

COOK'S TIP
Try to find Comice or Anjou pears - the recipe is best made with slightly underripe fruit.

Spiced Peach Crumble

INGREDIENTS

TOPPING
1 cup all-purpose flour
¼ teaspoon ground cinnamon
¼ teaspoon ground allspice
1 cup rolled oats
1 cup light brown sugar
½ cup butter

3 pounds ripe but firm peaches, peeled,
pitted and sliced
4 tablespoons sugar
½ teaspoon ground cinnamon
1 teaspoon lemon juice
plain yogurt or whipped cream,
to serve (optional)

SERVES 6

49

1 Preheat the oven to 375°F.

2 Make the topping. Sift the flour and spices into a bowl. Add the oats and sugar and stir to combine. Cut in the butter until the mixture resembles coarse crumbs.

3 Toss the peaches with the sugar, cinnamon and lemon juice. Put the fruit in an 8- or 9-inch diameter baking dish.

4 Scatter the topping over the fruit in an even layer. Bake the crumble for 30–35 minutes, until golden, and serve warm, with a bowl of yogurt on the side.

VARIATIONS
Use apricots or nectarines instead of peaches.

Clementines in Cinnamon Caramel

INGREDIENTS

8-12 clementines
1 cup sugar
1¼ cups boiling water
2 cinnamon sticks
2 tablespoons orange-flavored liqueur
¼ cup shelled pistachios
plain yogurt or crème fraîche,
to serve (optional)

SERVES 4–6

2 Gently heat the sugar in a pan until it melts and turns a rich golden brown. Immediately turn off the heat to prevent the caramel from darkening.

3 Covering your hand with a dish towel, add 1¼ cups of boiling water (the mixture will bubble and may spit). Bring slowly to a boil, stirring until the caramel has dissolved. Add the cinnamon sticks and the strips of peel, then simmer for 5 minutes. Stir in the liqueur.

4 Cool the syrup for 10 minutes, then pour it over the clementines. Cover and chill overnight.

1 Pare the rind from two clementines using a vegetable peeler, taking care to remove none of the white pith. Cut the rind into fine strips and set aside. Peel the clementines, as cleanly as you can, and put them in a bowl.

5 Blanch the nuts in boiling water for a few seconds. Drain, cool and remove the dark outer skin from each nut. Chop the pistachios and scatter over the clementines; serve the dish immediately, either as it is or with yogurt.

Pineapple Wedges with Allspice & Lime

INGREDIENTS

1 medium-size ripe pineapple
1 lime
1 tablespoon dark brown sugar
1 teaspoon ground allspice

SERVES 4

52

1 Cut the pineapple lengthwise into quarters and remove the core from each piece.

2 Loosen the flesh by sliding a knife between the flesh and the skin. Cut the flesh into slices, leaving it on the skin. Push alternate slices left and right, as illustrated in the main picture.

3 Remove a few shreds of rind from the lime. Cut the fruit in half and squeeze out all the juice. Sprinkle all the pineapple pieces with the sugar,  fresh lime juice, allspice and rind shreds. Serve immediately, or cover and chill for 1 hour.

VARIATION

For a quick hot dish, place the pineapple slices on a baking sheet, sprinkle them with the lime juice, sugar and allspice and place them under a hot broiler for 3-4 minutes, or until golden. Sprinkle with the shreds of lime zest and serve.

Spiced Red Fruit Compôte

INGREDIENTS

4 ripe red plums, quartered
2 cups strawberries, halved
2 cups raspberries
2 tablespoons light brown sugar
2 tablespoons cold water
1 cinnamon stick
3 pieces star anise
6 cloves
plain yogurt or ricotta cheese, to serve

SERVES 4

1 Place the plums, strawberries and raspberries in a heavy saucepan with the sugar and water.

2 Add the cinnamon stick, star anise and cloves to the pan and heat gently, without boiling, until the sugar dissolves and the juices run from the fruit.

3 Cover the pan and let the fruit infuse over very low heat for about 5 minutes. Remove the whole spices from the compôte before serving warm with yogurt or ricotta cheese.

Baked Treats

Spiced Date & Walnut Cake

INGREDIENTS

2¼ cups whole-wheat
self-rising flour
2 teaspoons pumpkin pie spice
scant 1 cup chopped dates
½ cup chopped walnuts
4 tablespoons sunflower oil
½ cup dark brown sugar
1¼ cups milk
walnut halves, to decorate

SERVES 10–12

55

1 Preheat the oven to 350°F. Grease and line a 2-pound loaf pan with waxed paper or non-stick parchment paper.

2 Sift together the flour and spice, adding any bran left in the sifter. Stir in the dates and walnuts.

3 Combine the oil, sugar and milk, then stir evenly into the dry ingredients. Spoon into the prepared pan and arrange the walnut halves on top of the mixture.

4 Bake the cake for 45–50 minutes, or until golden brown and firm. Turn out the cake, remove the lining paper and let cool on a wire rack. Wrap well in plastic and let sit for 2 days before cutting.

VARIATION
For a delicious alternative, try using pecans in place of the walnuts in this cake.

Apple & Cinnamon Crumble Cake

INGREDIENTS

3 large cooking apples
½ teaspoon ground cinnamon
1 cup butter
scant 1¼ cups sugar
4 eggs
4 cups self-rising flour

CRUMBLE TOPPING
¼ cup light brown sugar
1¼ cups all-purpose flour
1 teaspoon ground cinnamon
⅔ cup dried coconut
½ cup butter

SERVES 10–12

1 Preheat the oven to 350°F. Grease a 10-inch round cake pan or a shallow 8-inch square cake pan and line the bottom with wax paper. Make the crumble topping. Mix together the sugar, flour, cinnamon and coconut in a bowl, rub in the butter with your fingertips until the mixture resembles coarse crumbs, and set aside.

2 Peel and core the cooking apples, then grate them coarsely. Place them in a bowl, sprinkle with the cinnamon, toss to coat and set aside.

3 Cream the butter and sugar in a bowl with an electric mixer (or use a food processor), until light and fluffy. Beat in the eggs, one at a time, beating well after each addition. Sift in half the flour, mix well, then add the remaining flour and stir until the batter is smooth.

4 Spread half the cake batter evenly over the base of the prepared pan. Spoon the apples on top and scatter with half the crumble topping. Spread with the remaining cake batter, then top with the remaining crumble topping.

5 Bake for 1 hour and 10 minutes—1 hour and 20 minutes, covering the cake with foil if it browns too quickly. Cool in the pan for about 5 minutes, before turning out on a wire rack to cool.

COOK'S TIP

To make the topping in a food processor, add all the ingredients and process for a few seconds until the mixture resembles coarse crumbs.

Ginger Cookies

INGREDIENTS

2¼ cups all-purpose flour
2 teaspoons ground ginger
½ teaspoon grated nutmeg
1 teaspoon ground cinnamon
2 teaspoons baking powder
½ teaspoon salt
½ cup butter, softened
½ cup margarine, softened
½ cup light brown sugar
1 cup granulated sugar
⅓ cup molasses
1 egg

MAKES 36

1 Preheat the oven to 325°F. Line and grease 2–3 baking sheets. Sift the flour, spices, baking powder and salt together three times.

2 Cream the butter and margarine, brown sugar and half the granulated sugar until fluffy. Beat in the molasses, egg and flour. Chill until firm.

3 Place the remaining granulated sugar in a shallow dish. Roll tablespoonfuls of the dough into balls, then roll the balls in the sugar to coat them well.

4 Place the balls 2 inches apart on the prepared sheets and flatten slightly. Bake for 12–15 minutes, until golden around the edges but soft in the middle. Let sit for 5 minutes before cooling on a rack.

VARIATION

To make Gingerbread Men, increase the flour by ¼ cup. Roll out the dough and cut out shapes. Bake and frost.

Pepper-Spice Cookies

INGREDIENTS

1¼ cups all-purpose flour
½ cup cornstarch
2 teaspoons baking powder
½ teaspoon ground cardamom
½ teaspoon ground cinnamon
½ teaspoon grated nutmeg
½ teaspoon ground ginger
½ teaspoon ground allspice
½ teaspoon salt
½ teaspoon ground black pepper
1 cup butter or margarine,
softened
½ cup light brown sugar
½ teaspoon vanilla extract
1 teaspoon finely grated lemon rind
¼ cup whipping cream
¾ cup ground almonds

MAKES 48

1 Preheat the oven to 350°F. Sift the flour, cornstarch, baking powder, spices, salt and ground pepper into a bowl. Set aside.

2 With a mixer or in a food processor, cream the butter or margarine and brown sugar until light and fluffy. Beat in the vanilla and lemon rind.

3 With the mixer on low speed, add the spicy flour mixture alternately with the cream, beginning and ending with flour. Stir in the ground almonds.

4 Shape ¾-inch balls from the dough and place 1 inch apart on ungreased baking sheets. Bake for 15–20 minutes. Transfer to a wire rack to cool.

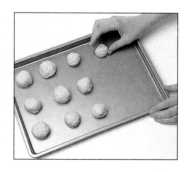

Cardamom & Saffron Tea Loaf

INGREDIENTS

pinch of saffron strands
3 cups lukewarm milk
2 tablespoons butter
8 cups all-purpose flour
2 packets easy-blend dried yeast
3 tablespoons sugar
6 cardamom pods, split open and
seeds extracted
⅔ cup raisins
2 tablespoons honey, plus extra
for brushing
1 egg, beaten

SERVES 10–12

1 Crush the saffron into a cup containing a little of the warm milk and let infuse for 5 minutes.

2 Rub the butter into the flour, then mix in the yeast, the sugar and the cardamom seeds (these may need rubbing to get them apart). Stir in the raisins.

3 Beat all the remaining milk with the honey and egg, then mix this into the flour mixture with the saffron milk. Stir well until a firm dough is formed (you may not need all the milk; this will depend on the flour). Turn out the dough and knead it on a lightly floured board for 5 minutes.

4 Return the dough to the mixing bowl, cover with oiled plastic wrap and leave in a warm place until doubled in size – this could take 1–3 hours, depending on the room temperature.

5 Grease a 2-pound loaf pan. Turn the dough out onto a floured board again, punch it down, knead for 3 minutes, then shape it into a fat roll and fit it into the loaf pan.

6 Cover with a sheet of lightly oiled clear plastic and let stand in a warm place until the dough begins to rise again. Preheat the oven to 400°F.

7 Bake the loaf for 25 minutes until golden brown and firm on top. Turn out of the pan and place on a wire rack. As the loaf cools, brush the top with honey. Slice the tea loaf when cold.

Pumpkin Spice Bread

INGREDIENTS

2 teaspoons ground cinnamon
1 teaspoon ground ginger
1 teaspoon ground allspice
¼ teaspoon ground cloves
5½ cups flour
1 teaspoon salt
2 packets easy-blend dried yeast
generous 1 cup sugar
1 cup cooked or canned pumpkin
½ cup butter, melted
½ cup warm milk
1 cup warm water
½ cup pecans, finely chopped

MAKES 1 LOAF

1 Combine the spices. Put 2 teaspoons of the spice mix in a mixing bowl. Add the flour, salt, yeast and ½ cup of the sugar. Mash the pumpkin with 3 tablespoons of the butter and all the milk. Add this to the flour mixture with enough of the water to make a dough. Knead on a floured surface until smooth. Return the dough to the clean bowl, cover and let rise in a warm place for about 1½ hours, or until doubled in bulk.

2 Punch the dough down and knead it briefly, then divide it into three equal pieces. Roll each piece into an 18-inch-long rope. Cut each rope into 18 equal pieces, then roll each piece into a ball.

3 Grease a 10-inch ring or tube pan. Stir the remaining sugar into the remaining spice mixture. Roll each ball in turn in the remaining melted butter, then in the sugar and spice mixture.

4 Arrange all the dough balls in the prepared pan in staggered rows, in more than one layer, if necessary. Sprinkle the balls with the chopped nuts as you work.

5 Preheat the oven to 350°F. Cover the pan and let stand in a warm place until the dough begins to rise again, then bake for 55 minutes. Cool in the pan for 20 minutes, then turn out onto a wire rack. Serve the bread warm.

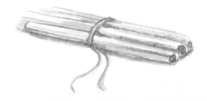

Index